for Bernie; Fred and Loan, Wendy, Leslie and Charlie, and also Rafael; and Molly, George, Mai Ly and Cody

Many thanks to everyone who walked with me:
Bernie, Leslie, George, Marice, Maile, Ann and Jess...
as well as Joyce Fishman, Ginger Birdsall, Gwen
Reichert, Jean Dana, Linda Liebes, Susan Shaffer,
Sally Foster, Mary King, Marilyn Massa,
Linda Hosken, Norma Tannenbaum, and
also to Mike Sugarman, who accompanied
me up Russian Hill one evening and gave
me a moment of fame on the radio. I loved
your company and insights, all of you.

Finally, heartfelt gratitude to
Leslie, Mary, Marice,
Audrey Sherlock and
Liz Greenberg for
doing the tedious,
arduous job of proofreading
and editing. You are saints.

TABLE OF CONTENTS

A WALKER'S SKETCHBOOK

OF

SAN FRANCISCO

A guide to its streets
plus 20 great walks

by Eleanor Burke

left: The Haas-Lilienthal House, Pacific Heights
cover: Vallejo and Jones Street, Russian Hill

Published by
Versa Press
1465 Spring Bay Road
East Peoria, Illinois 61611
Printed in Peoria
September 2016

ISBN 978-0-692-78030-5

A Walker's Sketchbook of San Francisco
A Guide to its Streets plus 20 Great Walks

drawings and text by
Eleanor Burke
egburke@earthlink.net

SAFETY NOTICE: My experience as a walker has been that the streets are
very safe to walk in the daytime hours. However, that does not mean you
shouldn't be aware of situations that might be risky. Take care to notice
your surroundings. My best advice is to be friendly and talk to people;
in that case, you are more than likely to find they will be friendly back.
But do be alert as you walk. This is a city, not a sanctuary.

INTRODUCTION

2015 was not a good year for farmers, but it was terrific for walkers. Sunny days at the end of 2014 were all the impetus I needed to get some much-needed exercise: I decided to walk every single street in San Francisco. The fact that I had no idea how many streets that entailed didn't matter, though I struggled in vain to find a map that definitively answered the question. The city is under what seems to be perpetual construction, with streets being added and subtracted almost daily, especially in neighborhoods like Mission Bay and Hunters Point. Nevertheless, I set out Jan 1, 2015 with the best maps I could gather and began to walk. I finished in mid-November, having walked 2,289 streets and alleys, all that I could find, over 700 miles. Not bad for a 77-year-old grandmother with an iffy knee and cranky hips.

This book is a visual record of what I came across on my walks. I talked to dozens of people, got invited into a film editor's studio in North Beach, took a "tour" of a sewer flusher's new truck in Eureka Valley, joined in the Russian Evangelical Church service on Balboa Street, discovered art in unlikely corners of the city, found churches of more denominations than I knew existed. En route I stopped in cafes and restaurants of amazing ethnic variety. On almost every walk I felt I could have been traveling abroad.

My strategy in walking the streets was to walk from point A to point B, then take public transportation back to the start. Muni made that wonderfully efficient and easy.

My purpose in doing this book is to encourage everyone who can walk to get out and explore this endlessly fascinating city. It is safe for daytime walkers: the single anxious moment I felt in all the 700+ miles was when I got swarmed by bees in Brooks Park. Luckily, I wasn't stung.

DANGER UNDERWATER OBSTRUCTIONS

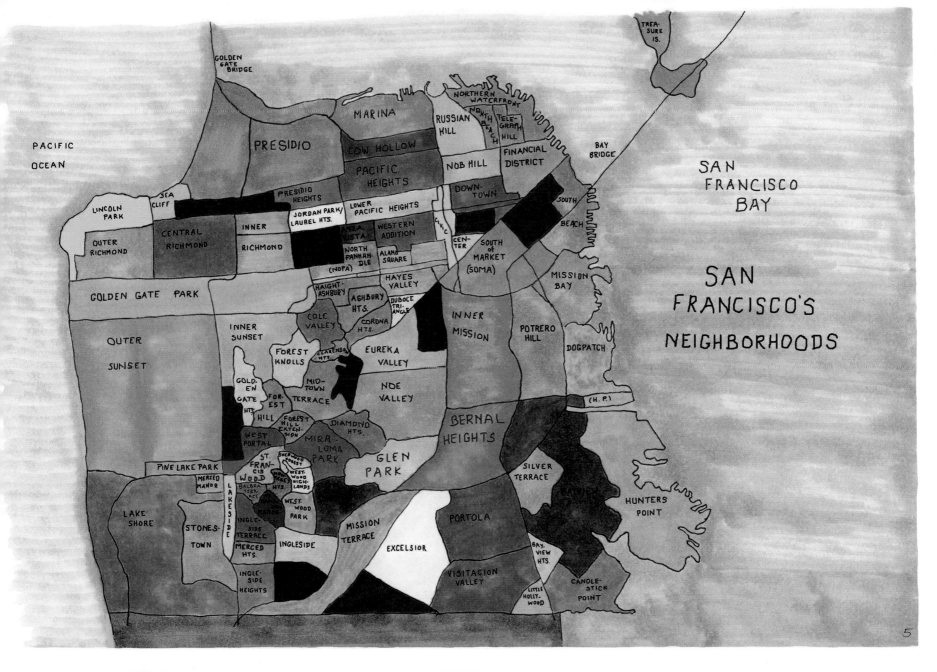

NORTH BEACH

I decided to start walking in North Beach, close to where I live, because I didn't know whether I'd be able to do what I'd envisioned. Ever hopeful, I set out on a beautiful New Year's Day, 2015 from Washington Square. A couple of blocks later, I came across this delicately graceful hotel and restaurant built by A.P. Giannini in 1886. After the '06 earthquake and fire, he generously sheltered homeless people here until they had housing again.

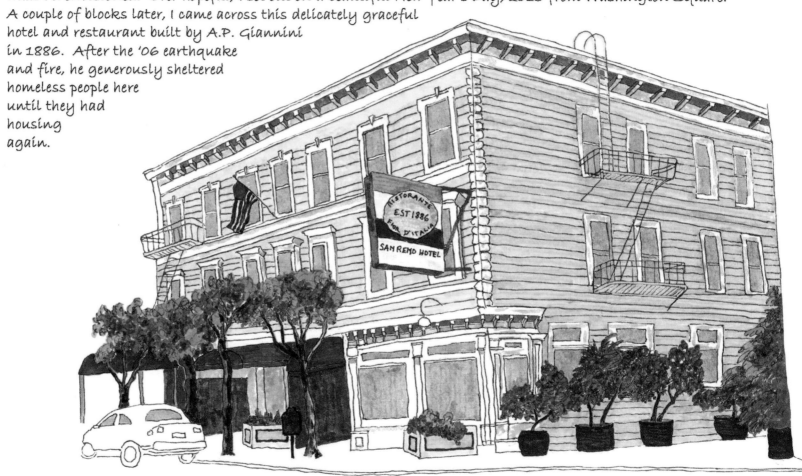

NORTH BEACH:

The Maybeck Building on the right is on Stockton Street. Though I'd passed by it many times, I never noticed it until my first day of walking. As I stood at the entrance, happy to have found a new treasure, a fellow walked up to me and invited me inside to his office/studio. A gracious, friendly man, he turned out to be a film editor. A great first day of walking!

There is no shortage of saloons in North Beach, many of which are colorful and historic. This one on the left caught my eye as I was having lunch next door.

NORTH BEACH: a bar with a sense of humor

Lots of watering holes in North Beach, and on any given day, something to celebrate.

MON. THRU FRI. 1PM-7PM
4.00 ALL PINTS & WELL DRINKS
FREE POOL & POPCORN
VOTED #1 HAPPY HOUR
By Betty Ford Clinic

HAPPY HOUR
4pm 9pm
BUY 1 GET 1
draft beers
well cocktails
7 DAYS A WEEK

But North Beach is not all bars and revelers. It's a neighborhood with people living in it, walking their dogs and enjoying sober conversations with friends. The old Italian flavor lingers, though Chinese influences are spreading north from Chinatown.

NORTH BEACH

Here's a local window with a warning...

On the corner of Broadway and Columbus, the west edge of Chinatown, this North Beach building celebrates its musical history. The book "sculptures" on wires above the street add to the visual impact.

TELEGRAPH HILL

One of the city's most scenic and historic neighborhoods, Telegraph Hill awes the visitor, even a native like me. Alta Street perches precariously on the hill above Montgomery Street, offering stunning views of the bay, historic houses and the torturous climbs.

When ships came into San Francisco Bay during the Gold Rush, sailors typically jumped ship to find their fortune in the hills. Captains needing ballast for outgoing vessels then used rock dynamited from beneath Alta Street. Of course, this caused problems with the stability of the hill, which continually collapsed onto Montgomery Street. People living in the houses on Alta Street were also in grave danger. At one point the mayor banned dynamiting, but clever lawbreakers simply waited until the 4th of July, when the noise from fireworks covered up the explosions, so the stability problem persisted.

TELEGRAPH HILL

You can't say Telegraph Hill dwellers don't have a sense of humor. This mural sits on the top of the hill, at the intersection of Alta and Montgomery Streets.

Coit Tower at the top of Telegraph Hill is its crown jewel, Lillie Coit's homage to her beloved fire department. Arthur Brown, who designed City Hall, was the architect. The murals inside are the result of the Depression-era W.P.A. that paid artists to paint murals in various parts of the city. Those inside Coit Tower are especially memorable, and on Wednesdays the City Guides give free tours of the murals behind the locked doors that go upstairs.

After walking North Beach and Telegraph Hill, I realized I could indeed walk the city: onward to the rest of the 2,289 streets!

CHINATOWN

Chinatown is densely populated, but even when families move out to other neighborhoods where they can have more space, they still come back often to shop and meet with those they left behind.

On the right is a housing project with a mural that depicts life in this venerable neighborhood. Laundry on fire escapes is part of the landscape.

CHINATOWN

People congregate in Chinatown to participate in morning exercises in Washington Square Park or shop for produce on Stockton Street.

CHINATOWN

Life on the streets of Chinatown
is endlessly fascinating,
like being in a foreign
country. You can
listen to a street
musician or
watch a fortune
cookie maker
or visit a
temple or
un herbal
   medicine
    shop, where
     you can
      get your
       ailments
        diagnosed
         and then
          cured
           with
            plants
            or deer
            horns or
         maybe things
       you've never
      seen before.

FINANCIAL DISTRICT

Walk down the canyons
between the huge build-
ings in the financial
district and look up
at the different shapes
and colors. It all seems
so very substantial.

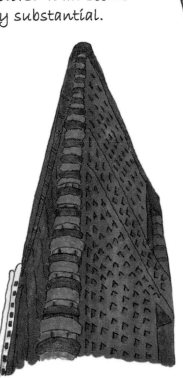

But the financial district is really all about the people who work there, go to school there, even live there. The Mechanics' Institute Library at the foot of Post Street is venerable: a library, a cultural event center and even a chess club. I belong to this library and use it as a place to sit down and read when I'm exhausted by the downtown throngs.

The nun on the right works at Notre Dame des Victoires, a church on Bush Street and a school next door, entrance on Pine Street. She is keeping the place at its spiffy best.

DOWNTOWN

Sam's has been around since about 1867, but I first ate there when Bernie and I were young marrieds, back in the early '60s. It was a treat to feast on abalone at Sam's, along with limestone lettuce salad. The zabaglione dessert made the whole experience memorable. Now, years later, it is still special, but minus the abalone and with new owners.

Foley's, on O'Farrell Street, is more of an Irish pub than a restaurant.

SAM'S GRILL

BELDEN
(60 00)
ONE WAY

Time For a Pint!

FOLEY'S

19

RUSSIAN HILL

This is the scene at the top of Russian Hill. A huge, modern Eichler looms above the low-rise Willis Polk-designed homes. It seems an appropriate challenge for an "old" neighborhood like this one: how to deal with a growing population in an already-densely packed urban area without destroying the history and culture of what was there before.

I live on this hill, steps away from this scene, so I'm reminded daily of the tension between past and present.

On Russian Hill it is not uncommon to see a film crew at work. Maybe this will be the next <u>Mrs. Doubtfire</u>?

21

COW HOLLOW

I found this plaque on a Filbert Street house in Cow Hollow.

This charming, almost fairy tale-like house at the end of Green Street was used in the film <u>The Princess Diaries</u>.

COW HOLLOW
(and SOUTH OF
MARKET)

Transportation problems in the city have given rise to the much-disputed "Google buses" - really a generic term for a vehicle getting employees to work. Ironically, many tech workers live now in San Francisco and commute to the peninsula, dramatically reversing decades-long patterns. These buses and mini-buses often usurp Muni pick-up spots while they wait for riders. Muni then just has to cool its heels until curb space becomes available again. On the other hand, these buses have taken hundreds of cars off the already-packed freeways during commute hours.

The Art Deco style of the Presidio movie theater on Chestnut Street below is typical of much of this neighborhood, built largely in the 1930s. Chestnut is a full-service shopping street with a small supermarket, a pharmacy, a couple of banks, good places to eat or linger over a cup of coffee - and a bookstore.

The sign on the building next to the Wells Fargo Bank made me smile.

Shopping on Sacramento
Street in Presidio Heights:

intimate boutiques
punctuated by upscale
restaurants

THE PRESIDIO

In the National Cemetery in the Presidio you will find graves of people who fought in every conflict in our history, that is, until recent years. Now the cemetery is full. But it is still a fascinating history lesson to walk around the tombstone monument.

The view of the city from a bench on the path out to Fort Point is really lovely.

PRESIDIO

Sea Scouts Honor Guard on Memorial Day, 2015

The brown pelican
is a lucky bird:
his species was
endangered
just a few
years ago,
but now,
protected
by law,
is thriving.
It's a great
story.

THE PRESIDIO

On Sundays from March to November the field in front of
the old Montgomery Street Barracks becomes a gourmet
picnic area. Off the Grid trucks line up on the sides,
serving everything from salads to paella to ice cream.
People bring their kids and dogs and folding chairs,
and the air is full of frisbees and beach balls.

THE PRESIDIO

In 2015 the new Doyle Drive was completed, a boon to those who love this national park because traffic largely out of sight now flows   through these air-conditioned tunnels.

PACIFIC HEIGHTS

This Pacific Heights woman
had two charming escorts
for her morning walk
through the neighborhood.

NOPA
(North of the
Panhandle)
is actually
an old
neighborhood
now
punctuated
by
modern
architecture.

631

GOLDEN GATE PARK: Before the Richmond District was all built up with houses, a railroad brought weekenders out here to this station along Fulton Street. A visit here is a return to the past, a time when the park was remote from downtown and most people didn't yet have automobiles.

GOLDEN GATE PARK

As I walked around Stow Lake, the birds relaxing on the shoreline ignored me...

...as did the early morning runners competing in a race that ended near the Great Highway.

OCEAN BEACH

From the Cliff House at the north end of Ocean Beach you can look down the coastline to San Mateo County. The western edge of Golden Gate Park is visible along with Beach Chalet and the Dutch windmill.

The bright colors of these houses along the Great Highway are the perfect antidote to the gray fog that often hangs over them.

CIVIC CENTER

This is one of at least eighteen neighborhood farmers' markets in the city, this one open on Wednesdays and Sundays starting at 7 a.m. Every day except Monday and Friday a farmers' market is open somewhere in San Francisco. The oldest is on Alemany Boulevard, the newest at UCSF in Mission Bay. They are deservedly popular.

In the shadow of City Hall these fellows were loitering where they shouldn't be. Lots of signs here.

CIVIC CENTER

One day I saw these protestors in front of the Phillip Burton Federal Building and U.S. Court House on Golden Gate Avenue. It turns out that every Thursday at noon they gather to show their opposition to our participation in the various wars in the Middle East. We chatted for a while before I left them, in awe of their passion and commitment.

LOWER POLK STREET

In Frank Norris's novel about early San Francisco, the main character is a dentist named McTeague. This part of our history is now commemorated by a lively bar in Polk Gulch.

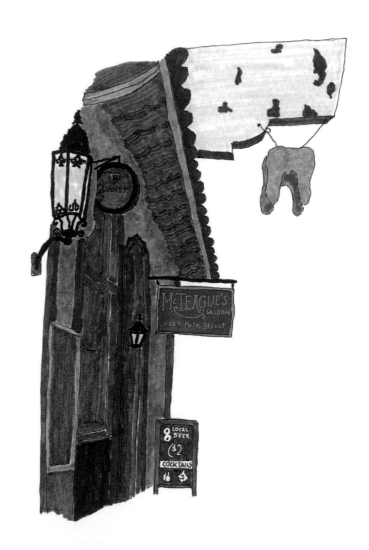

THE TENDERLOIN

The origin of this neighborhood's name is shrouded in myth: it may have come from a similar 'hood in New York City or it may be that the area, which has always been rough and tumble, offered police extra pay for working in it; hence they could pay for more expensive cuts of meat. No one seems to know for sure. The Glide Foundation provides great services, such as free meals for the homeless, computer training, child care, job skills training, legal services, mentoring youth and more. In June 2015 Warren Buffett auctioned off lunch with himself at a Glide benefit, raising $3.4 million for the Foundation. Cecil Williams, pastor at Glide until 1999 and still exerting strong influence, has largely been responsible for the success of this institution.

THE TENDERLOIN

Hospitality House and the Compass Center on Leavenworth and Golden Gate provide services for people in The Tenderloin, and it was impressive to see the variety of help they offer, from tutoring kids to counseling to job finding and drug rehabilitation.

The Tenderloin has become a haven for immigrants from Southeast Asia, especially Cambodians and Vietnamese. A well-run child care center in the neighborhood provides much-needed services for these kids and their families.

The Cambodian Battambang Market is a testament to the multi-cultural makeup of the area.

WESTERN
ADDITION

These guys were hanging out on Fillmore Street on a cool day.

The stones in the Fillmore Street sidewalks commemorate its illustrious past, especially its jazz musicians. Some not very successful efforts have been made to restore that legacy.

CATHEDRAL HILL

The abolitionist Thomas Starr King came to San Francisco from Boston in 1860. Here he eloquently and persuasively preached to have California join the Northern side in the Civil War. Lincoln credited him with saving the Union. Unfortunately, King died before the war was over so he never got to see the fruit of his efforts.

Above is the intersection of Geary and Franklin with St. Mary's Cathedral overlooking the wide swath that became the Geary Expressway in the '60s. During a contentious redevelopment period then hundreds of mostly black families were uprooted.

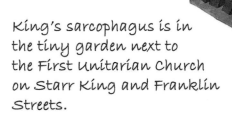

King's sarcophagus is in the tiny garden next to the First Unitarian Church on Starr King and Franklin Streets.

JAPANTOWN

Walk around Japan-
town to get a sense
of life there, its tra-
ditional aspects as
well as contemporary
activities such as shopping
in a Japanese grocery store like
the one below. I like the store at
Sutter and Buchanan. I buy sushi
and sashimi there, but the real treat
is the bakery, which sells the same
coffee crunch cake that we used to get
at Blum's sixty years ago. My mouth
is watering.

**To learn about the neigh-
borhood's history, don't miss
the stands of posters scattered
around, especially the ones on
Webster between Geary and
Post that describe the Japanese
internment during World
War II.**

44

JAPANTOWN

Several Japanese-style temples and a former Jewish Orthodox synagogue in this neighborhood indicate its spiritual and ethnic history. Before it became Japantown, it had a substantial Jewish population, who left after the '06 earthquake. Then the Japanese, who had been living mostly in Chinatown and south of Market, moved in. They were there until 1942, when the entire community was sent to internment camps, mostly in Utah (see walk at the end). Today most of the Japanese in the neighborhood are senior citizens.

This former synagogue is now part of the Kokoro Senior Community, but its historic facade, partly a copy of the Doge's Palace in Venice, remains.

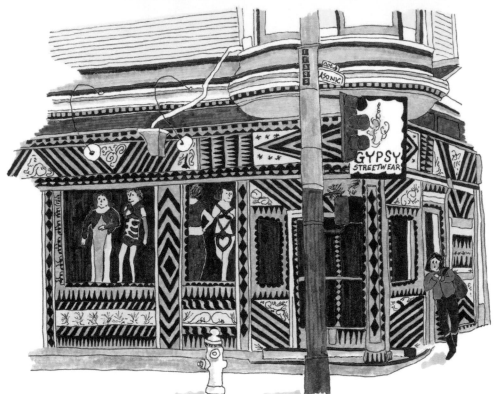

THE HAIGHT-ASHBURY

Famous because of its role as a haven for counterculture kids and dope deals in the '60s, the Haight today is much more conventional, though vestiges of those turbulent days remain.

Good idea: Walk over to Huckleberry House at 1 Broderick Street, a shelter for runaway and homeless kids that opened in 1967 during the Summer of Love. During the '60s and early '70s, Mayor Alioto tried many times, without success, to shut it down. It's still there, offering a variety of services to 11-17 year-olds in need of help.

A walk along Huight Street shows how imaginative shop owners can be.

Yet the neighborhood still has its serious side: The Haight-Ashbury Free Clinic continues to treat kids who have overdosed on drugs, and Huckleberry House offers counseling to them as well. But the infamous Charles Manson, who lived in the neighborhood with his harem before he went on a killing rampage in Los Angeles, is gone, and a Whole Foods Market is well-established.

The DUBOCE TRIANGLE is an enclave near the center of the city, tucked in under the slopes of Buena Vista Park and the Castro/Eureka Valley areas.

The meticulously restored and landscaped Victorians, the cafes with street seating, often sheltered from wind and fog, AND this lovely parklet right on the side-walk on Noe and 15th Streets make this neighborhood special.

MARKET STREET:

Walking down Market Street is like being in a street car museum. A few years ago the city started buying up old street cars from all over the world, restoring them and then putting them into service. Riding on one of the bone-jarring cars is an adventure. Look on the street car to see where it's from.

THE CASTRO

The intersection of 18th and Castro Streets here with the rainbow colors painted right on the crosswalk is the heart of the Castro. If you walk around this neighborhood, you will find the colors everywhere. A strong sense of verbal and visual humor pervades this area.

THE CASTRO

Walking through the Castro means
being entertained by the unusual
as well as the traditional, like
this row of charming Victorian
homes. All are neatly aligned
on the steep hill, beautifully
dressed in a variety
of colors. They are
as San Francisco
as the cable cars
and the Golden
Gate Bridge are.

THE CASTRO:

The Castro Theater, built in 1922 by the Nasser brothers, theater entrepreneurs, still has its original organ, which a skilled organist often plays before the films start.

In November, 2015, we saw these iconic noir films, part of the annual Film Noir Festival, popular with film buffs from all over.

THE CASTRO

Shopping in The Castro is an entertainment form. It's not every day you come across businesses like Hand Job or Does Your Mother Know? or Hot and Hunky.
But there is another side to The Castro. A strong sense of social justice pervades the air here, largely thanks to the legacy of Harvey Milk, openly gay, who was killed along with Mayor Moscone in 1978 by former supervisor Dan White. Milk had run a photography store on Castro Street before he was elected supervisor from this district and fought for gay rights.

MID-MARKET

As part of a plan to rejuvenate the mid-Market area, the city encouraged businesses like Twitter to move its headquarters to 10th and Market. The fancy grocery store on the ground floor is worth a visit, though its ridiculous prices seem not to be drawing crowds,

MID-MARKET

There is nothing like a beautiful mural to spiff up a seedy-looking section of town. This one of the Magi bringing gifts does the job.

SOUTH OF MARKET - the grim picture:
The city is changing, growing, expanding - and housing prices
are going higher than skyscrapers. The scene is one of never-
ending noise and disruption for everyone. Streets are
often blocked and traffic seems at a constant standstill.
The growth of the lauded tech
industry is
probably the
main reason for this
chaos, proving that
nothing good comes
for free.

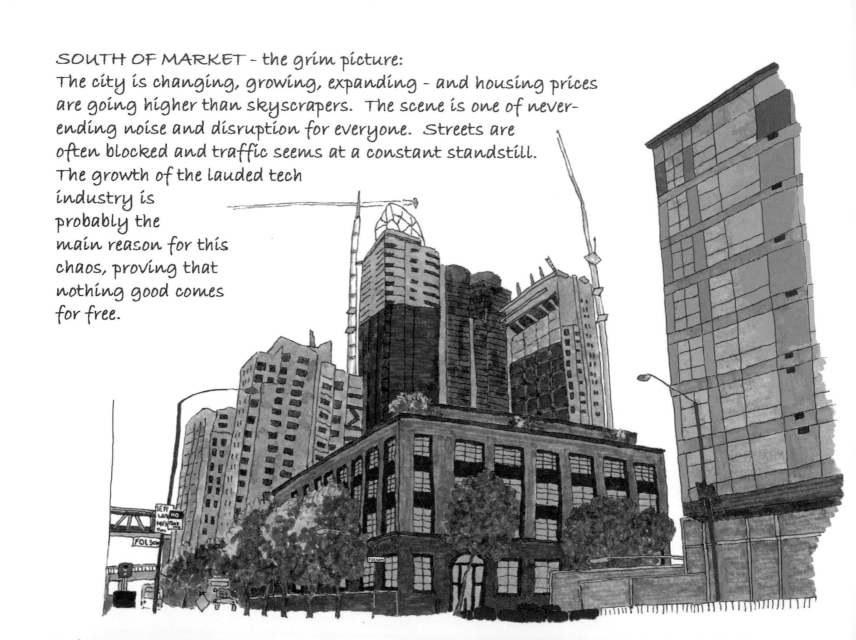

SOMA: (South of Market): On 5th Street off Brannan you will see this mural depicting a failed dream with homeless people sitting underneath, seeming to validate the picture. Then, as if to accentuate the divide, guys are bicycling to their jobs or parking their cars in the lot before heading to their offices.

The Candlestick Cove condos above are a welcome addition to an otherwise bleak landscape on the fringe of Hunters Point, but they also present a problem for the people in Little Hollywood since access is easiest through their quiet little neighborhood.

On the right is one of the many apartment complexes in SOMA (South of Market), transforming the neighborhood into a place where families can live.

SOMA

The Holy Cow on Folsom near 11th Street welcomes thirsty walkers.

Below some arrestingly unusual architecture in one of the alleys in this area.

Both are hard to pass by without stopping to look and enjoy.

SOMA - A martial arts class works out on a Sunday morning.

A Sunday morning ballet class,
in a SOMA warehouse on an
alley, distracted us from our walk.

61

MIRALOMA PARK

This is a family-oriented neighborhood for the most part with modest, well-maintained houses and gardens. Miraloma School on the left has an excellent reputation. The signs on the post do seem to indicate that its students know their place in the world.

MIRALOMA
PARK

Just because we San
Franciscans live in
an urban setting
doesn't mean we
lack wildlife.

The metal
and wood
sculptures
on Edge-
hill Drive
in this
upscale
neigh-
borhood
are as
amusing
as they
are unex-
pected.

100

NOE VALLEY

These dogs
at
Douglass
Park
focus
on
their
reward.

THE SUNSET

As I approached this intersection, I imagined myself driving a car or a bus, trying to figure out what I was supposed to do and when. Too many instructions given too fast, or maybe I am just getting old.

OCEAN BEACH

At the end of Taraval Street at the western edge of the city, just before you step into the icy waves of the Pacific, you come across Surfhenge, three giant mosaic sculptures designed by DPW landscape architect Martha Ketterer, with tile work done by Colette Crutcher. Ketterer's purpose was to combine the lightness and fragility of surfboards and sails with monumental weight and verticality, while Crutcher wanted to capture the ceaseless dance of the ocean and its creatures. Crutcher, along with Aileen Barr, also designed the famous mosaic stairs on 16th and Kirkham, the Hidden Garden stairs on 16th and Lawton and the Arelious Walker stairs in Hunters Point. The Balboa Streetscape sculptures at 34th and 39th Avenues on Balboa are hers also.

These fishermen, oblivious to sculptures, are hoping to haul in dinner from the surf.

67

Large lots with elegant homes in classical styles mark this neighborhood in the southwest area of the city. The one on the left, a Dutch Colonial house, has the gambrel roof that is typical of the style.

On the right is a Craftsman style house, popular in the years between 1905-1920, influenced by the arts and Crafts movement and even Asian architecture. Characteristics of this style are the low-pitched roof, a front porch, multi-paned windows, single dormers, brick piers, exposed rafter tails and beams under deep roof covers and knee braces (triangular supports).

*I recommend taking a walk through these southwestern neighborhoods - see walk #4 at the end.

THE EXCELSIOR

In spite of the distinguished-sounding street names (international universities like Oxford & Goettingen) and the international flavor of other street names (Peru, Madrid, Russia), this is an unpretentious, blue collar neighborhood. Historically the population here has been mostly Asian and Hispanic families as well as retired people.

But lately the population has begun to change a bit as young people find housing more affordable here than in the city's tonier neighborhoods.

McLaren Park, a huge, underused swath of open space, is on its eastern edge.

Murals are common here, whether on a grocery store or a freeway overpass.

POTRERO HILL

One sunny Sunday morning Bernie and I were ambling down DeHaro Street on Potrero Hill. Hearing music from the open doors of St. Gregory's Episcopal Church, affectionately called "The Church of the Dancing Saints" because of the murals on the walls of the circular church entry, we walked over to see what was going on. We stood at the door while the parishoners re-enacted the dance in the murals above. Everyone joined in, young and old, healthy and feeble. They invited us to join them, but I was too fascinated watching and taking photographs to draw from later on, and Bernie was too shy. I regret my hesitation, wish I had experienced this special event that takes place every Sunday on DeHaro and Mariposa, right across from the Anchor Steam Brewery.

I strongly recommend that you visit St. Gregory's on a Sunday morning - and don't be as shy as we were.

In the playground of a school on Potrero Hill that same Sunday morning, we came upon a hula class that treated us to a charming show.

BERNAL HEIGHTS

This is one of my very favorite neighborhoods in the city, full of gay and straight families with lots of children and dogs, enhanced by steps and winding streets - and terrific weather. People are out on the streets, talking with their neighbors. Precita Park on the right is well-used. The dog would love to be included in the fun.

BERNAL HEIGHTS houses are
modest, attractive and comfortable.
The neighborhood is like a village
within the city.

OUTER MISSION

The recycle line on DeWolf Street gets long early in the morning.

Balboa High School's early California architecture makes it look as if it belonged in Beverly Hills instead of this working class neighborhood. The murals of life in California are special. Balboa has the smallest student population of any other high school in the city.

Streets in Mission Terrace are mostly named after American Indian tribes, like Onondaga, Modoc, Seminole, Navajo, Oneida, etc.

MISSION TERRACE

The Royal Baking Company on Mission Street features a lovely mural of the Last Supper. On the right is an indication that they also provide baked goods for a girl's Quinceanera celebration, the ceremony that marks her 15th birthday and thus her passage to womanhood in the Mexican culture.

OUTER MISSION: As it is everywhere else in the city, parking here is scarce.

In the OMI (Ocean View, Merced Heights, Ingleside) area on the southern edge of the city is this gem: 30 homes being built by Habitat for Humanity and sold at cost to lucky families. They are 3-bedroom/3-bath and 2-bedroom/2-bath single family homes. Labor is donated by local saints...

...including my brother-in-law.

NAACK INTERNS

KEEP OUT

PRIVATE KEEP OUT!

PARKMERCED/SAN FRANCISCO STATE UNIVERSITY

The high-rises are a relatively new part of the landscape as this entire area seems to be going up, towers replacing low-rise town homes. We used to live in Parkmerced in a lovely town home with a grassy common back yard and play areas for the kids. At least kids are still playing here.

LITTLE HOLLYWOOD

Tucked in between Bayshore Blvd. and the Bayshore Freeway on the southeastern edge of the city, this is its smallest neighborhood: it covers less than a square mile and has fewer than 1,000 residents. It is shaped like a pie with the pointed end of the triangle a road that goes under the freeway to Candlestick Cove on the other side. A Recology dump is on its south end, but this place is no dump; rather it is a quiet neighborhood with a peaceful park and well-kept houses built in the '20s and '30s that some said were pretty enough to be in Hollywood. Schlage Lock Company and Southern Pacific once provided jobs here, but they are long gone. Still, this is a close-knit community where people know each other and resist the change that the upscale town homes of Candlestick Cove has brought. Access to those town homes is mostly through Little Hollywood, where residents are trying to keep out buses, cars, stoplights, and anything else that disturbs their peace and quiet.

Bayview-Hunters Point is changing. In some ways, it's not changing fast enough, as seen in this derelict building in the old Navy shipyard land that is still contaminated by radioactive waste from World War II. The problem is that no one wants to pay for the expensive cleanup: not the feds (the Navy), not the state of California, not the city of San Francisco.

The more promising prospect involves the public housing complexes in the area. This one below, the Alice Griffith Community, was built in 1963 but is gradually becoming vacant as residents move to newer and nicer quarters elsewhere. Sitting behind a forbidding iron fence with a single entrance road and three speed bumps, Alice Griffith felt isolated from the beginning. It had no grocery stores, pharmacies or banks nearby. With new public housing complexes coming in, this bleak picture is changing.

The positive efforts are the houses and the public transit.
Now people live in new housing on cul-de-sacs, mostly
landscaped, conversing with neighbors on the street.
What is still needed are shopping facilities that include
supermarkets, pharmacies, banks, and, of course, a bookstore.

BAYVIEW

Above is some of the new Bayview housing that has dramatically upgraded the neighborhood.

On the left is a former eyesore that was transformed into art: a silo painted with a mural features a nautical theme. At night it is lit up to entertain drivers, even those on the nearby freeway. The structure is off 3rd Street just before you get to Cargo Way going south.

BAYVIEW

This young girl had just chased and caught a stray dog, which, of course, she wanted to keep. Immediately her mother appeared and said no. We didn't stay for the inevitable back and forth that was coming, but I wished her luck.

The street sign is a reminder that this neighborhood still has its problems: a bullet hole is a chilling warning that life here isn't yet as safe and secure as it ought to be.

HUNTERS POINT

One day as I was walking down Jamestown Avenue, I came across this sight: Candlestick Park was being demolished. Just two days later it was gone. A wave of nostalgia came over me as I thought of all the excitement I'd experienced at Candlestick Park watching Willie Mays, Willie McCovey, Juan Marichal, Joe Montana, Steve Young, all while I was listening to Russ Hodges and Lon Simmons on KSFO as I sat in our seats behind the first base dugout or in the end zone. Now we've moved on to AT&T Park, where it is usually warmer than it was at chilly Candlestick.

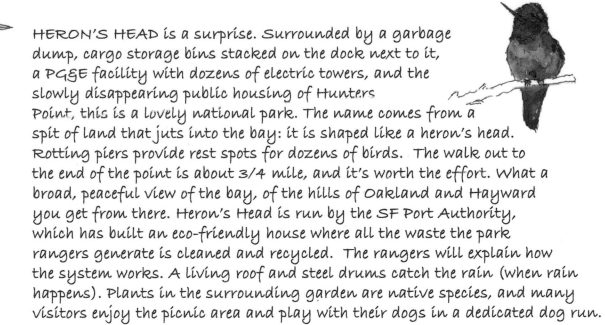

HERON'S HEAD is a surprise. Surrounded by a garbage dump, cargo storage bins stacked on the dock next to it, a PG&E facility with dozens of electric towers, and the slowly disappearing public housing of Hunters Point, this is a lovely national park. The name comes from a spit of land that juts into the bay: it is shaped like a heron's head. Rotting piers provide rest spots for dozens of birds. The walk out to the end of the point is about 3/4 mile, and it's worth the effort. What a broad, peaceful view of the bay, of the hills of Oakland and Hayward you get from there. Heron's Head is run by the SF Port Authority, which has built an eco-friendly house where all the waste the park rangers generate is cleaned and recycled. The rangers will explain how the system works. A living roof and steel drums catch the rain (when rain happens). Plants in the surrounding garden are native species, and many visitors enjoy the picnic area and play with their dogs in a dedicated dog run.

To get there, go south on 3rd Street and turn left on Evans to the end, where it becomes Jennings. Heron's Head is right there.

I've seen grebes, blue herons, egrets, oystercatchers, avocets, mallards, brown pelicans, and of course, the omnipresent gull.

(This is part of the 3rd Street walk described in the final section of this book.)

DOGPATCH

A great neighborhood for walking, Dog-patch has history and local color along with excellent eateries. In recent years, with the growing popularity of the city's southern neighborhoods with their easy access to the freeways going south to Sili-con Valley, Dogpatch has become trendy. Still, one sees vestiges of the old Dog-patch, like the Hells' Angels' head-quarters on Tennessee Street. Members of that formidable group are often at Just For You on 22nd Street, eating beignets. Lots of history here too, including the cottages on Minnesota Street that were built for $572 from catalog plans and have now been renovated and mostly enlarged.

The city's newest neighborhood lies along the bay just south of AT&T Park. Just a few years ago it was a blank canvas with a few derelict warehouses. Now it is UCSF's latest campus, with the Mark Benioff Children's Hospital and other medical facilities that include biotech research labs and a large open area that hosts a farmers' market every Wednesday, rain or shine.

Also part of the landscape is housing, lots of it. It ranges from "affordable" to low income to market rate. And of course, there are parking garages like the one above for people living and working here. A growing number of places where one can snack, dine, have a cup of coffee or shop for groceries are appearing as demand for them increases.

There is also a lovely walking trail here along the bay. And, of course, at the north end of 3rd Street sits the excellent home of the Giants, AT&T Park.

MISSION BAY

SOUTH BEACH

A busy walkway and thoroughfare along the bay, The Embarcadero offers art, some excellent architecture and great places to eat, like those below: On the left a statue of a chef perches on the lovely mansard roof above Boulevard Restaurant in the Audiffred Building. Below is our family favorite, Delancey Street, at The Embarcadero and Brannan. Delancey is special: Mimi Silbert, who co-founded it in 1971 with John Maher, does a heroic job of rehabilitating the ex-drug addicts and criminals who work for Delancey and live in the complex that they themselves built. We usually eat there before Giants' games and love the staff, on the road to a changed life. They are happy to tell you their individual stories if you ask.

SOUTH BEACH

When the Embarcadero Freeway was demolished after the '89 Loma Prieta earthquake, this promenade along the bay became a beautiful walk again.

Red's Java House has survived all efforts to tear it down and turn it into something larger, taller and more elegant. Locals love having a place to go for a plain hot dog and a cup of coffee. No Starbuck's here, just simple joe.

SOUTH BEACH - AT&T PARK

Opening day of the 2016 season in April was wonderful. Fans were full of hope and thrilled that the long winter off-season was over and that with spring come some great baseball games.

We were all thinking of the World Series Champion- ships the Giants had won in 2010, 2012 and 2014.

TREASURE
ISLAND

THE EMBARCADERO

It's an exercise in meditation to walk along The Embarcadero on a nice morning. On this particular morning, the fog was still hanging just above the water under the Bay Bridge, the air quite still. A lone fisherman was waiting patiently for some action from below, and the morning traffic had not yet grown to its usual roar.

A law-abiding bird if there ever was one, this Canada Goose was walking on Treasure Island one afternoon. Treasure Island, which is part of the city and county of San Francisco, was created in 1936-7 for the 1939 Golden Gate International Exposition. During World War II it was a naval base which hosted radioactive ships from the Bikini Atoll atomic tests that left part of the island contaminated.

Holy Trinity Greek Orthodox Church (left) was built in 1964, but its original version was erected in 1904 on 7th and Cleveland Streets. It is on Brotherhood way, joined by Congregation Beth Israel Judea, Calvary Armenian Church and the Lake Merced Church of Christ.

Below is a Pentecostal Samoan church on San Jose Avenue in Mission Terrace.

These churches as well as the ones on the following two pages testify to the rich cultural and ethnic diversity that San Francisco has.

SAMOAN
ASSEMBLY OF GOD

Below is the Molokan Church on Potrero Hill, a congregation whose members are outcasts from the traditional Russian Orthodox Church and considered heretical. The Molokans, or milk drinkers, have insisted since the late 1800s on drinking milk on holy days in defiance of a church prohibition against the practice. They came to SF and built a church on Carolina Street, where they still worship today, in Russian, of course.

On the right is the Burmese Baptist Church on Ottilia Street just over the line into Daly City adjacent to the Crocker-Amazon. I'm including it in this San Francisco book because it is Burmese and a few feet shouldn't matter.

93

WESTERN
ADDITION

DOMVS·DEI·SVB·TIT ꞏ SANCTAE CR

MACANG MONASTERY

I had a conversation with this monk
at the Tibetan/Chinese monastery
on Eddy Street. When I asked him
whether it was Chinese or Tibetan,
he replied that Buddha didn't know
the difference. The temple invites
visitors to come in and relax a
while.

94

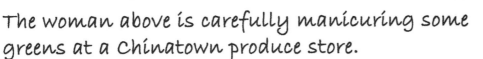

The woman above is carefully manicuring some greens at a Chinatown produce store.

The fellow on the right is a sewer flusher, friendly and eager to tell me about the brand new sewer flushing truck the city had just bought. That day he was working in Eureka Valley.

95

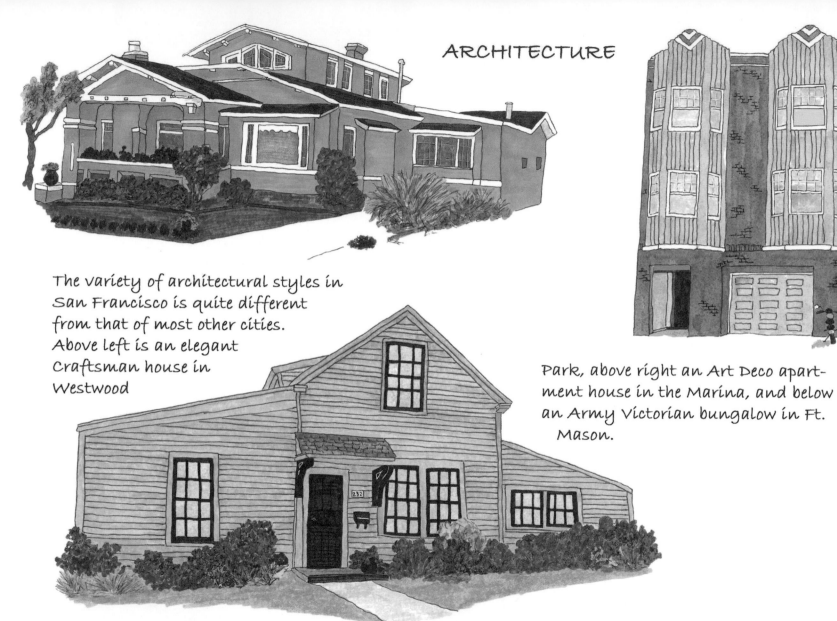

ARCHITECTURE

The variety of architectural styles in
San Francisco is quite different
from that of most other cities.
Above left is an elegant
Craftsman house in
Westwood

Park, above right an Art Deco apartment house in the Marina, and below
an Army Victorian bungalow in Ft.
Mason.

Lots of Giants and
Warriors fans in
San Francisco!

Modern and
traditional
styles exist
harmoniously
in the city.
On the right
is a Victorian
cottage in
Eureka
Valley,
below a
modern
condo
building
in the
Inner
Richmond
District.

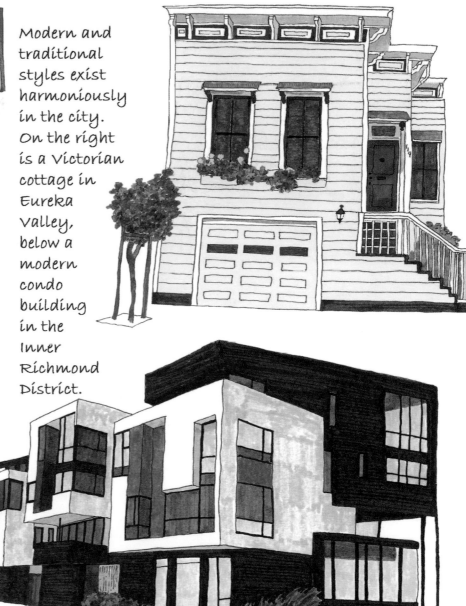

MURALS

Murals have become a distinct part of the San Francisco landscape, thanks mainly to Diego Rivera, who painted the one below, called Pan-American Unity. It hangs on the wall outside the City College of SF theater, and often a docent is there who will tell you all about it. In it you see Rivera himself, along with Frieda Kahlo, the Mexican artist known for her self-portraits. Two other remarkable Rivera murals adorn the walls at the City Club, 155 Sansome Street (Allegory of California) and the SF Art Institute, 800 Chestnut Street.

The dragon mural above is on Wentworth Alley in Chinatown.

Tim Pfleuger, well-known SF architect who designed 450 Sutter with its Mayan designs, the Pacific Coast Stock Exchange building at 155 Sansome, the Pacific Telegraph and Telephone Co. and the Colonial Revival Castro Theater, is also depicted in the mural on the right.

98

MURALS come in
many forms: On
the right is the
great swerve on
Upper Market
Street that
many drivers who
go by at speeds that exceed the speed limit miss.

Below left is a delightful mural oasis in a Mission District alley.

And below right is a brilliantly done mosaic stairway designed by Aileen Barr, who

helped design the mosaic
stairway at 16th and
Moraga. This one is
at the west end of
California Street,
off 32nd Avenue.
It was finished in
2015, inspired by
a couple of parents
of the Katherine
Delmar Burke
School next to it, a huge improve-
ment over the cold gray stairs
to Lincoln Park that the
tiles now cover.

WALK #1: Noriega Street in the Sunset

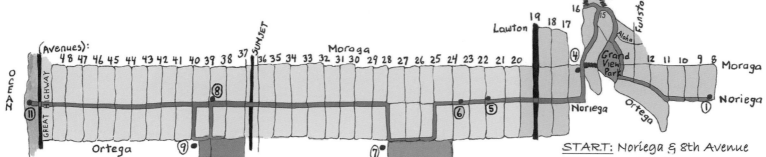

(Avenues): 48 47 46 45 44 43 42 41 40 39 38 37 SUNSET 36 35 34 33 32 31 30 29 28 27 26 25 24 23 22 21 20 Lawton 19 18 17 16 15 Aloha Funston 12 11 10 9 8 Moraga

OCEAN · GREAT HIGHWAY · Moraga · Ortega · Noriega · Grand View Park · Noriega

START: Noriega & 8th Avenue
END: Ocean Beach
DISTANCE: about 3 miles
RETURN: Get the 71 bus at 47th & Noriega, take it to 22nd and Judah (4 blks north of Noriega), get the N Judah street car east to 9th Ave, then take the 6 bus south to Noriega & walk 1 block to 8th Ave

<u>Do this walk on a sunny day!</u> Start at the top of Golden Gate Heights (1), follow route over to the 15th Ave steps (2) and the tiled Hidden Garden steps (3), then walk over 15th Ave to the tiled steps at 16th & Moraga (4). These stairways are exceptional! Stop at 22nd & Noriega for another good mosaic. Stop for a break at the House of Coffee (6), a neighborhood icon. Continue to the solar array on the roof of the reservoir (7). Don't miss Polly Ann's on 39th for an ice cream (8). Walk by the murals on the Sunset Library (9) and Giannini Middle School (10). End by dipping your feet in the sand and surf across the Great Highway (11) for a dose of refreshment. You've done well.

NOW THEN: This is the first of 20 walks that I particularly enjoyed and recommend that you take. Much is left out or overlooked, of course, but I think the range of walks covers most of the city. My way of walking is one-way; that is, I walk to a destination and then take public transportation (or Uber or Lyft) back to my starting point. The maps show the routes. Enjoy!!!

WALK #2: the RICHMOND
including Balboa and Fulton Streets and USF

START: Anza & Arguello
END: Cliff House
DISTANCE: 4+ miles
RETURN: 38 Geary to Arguello

house at 10th and Fulton

This route takes you through a chunk of the Richmond District. Follow the yellow route from Anza and Arguello. Stop first at the Columbarium, a fascinating cemetery of ashes with stories, photos, stained glass and more. Then continue to the USF campus off Parker. Take the walkway between Turk & Fulton, opposite McAllister, into the campus. Find Kalmanovitz Hall on the right, go inside to find a Renaissance-era church portal. Outside across the way is a lovely sunken area and the Gleeson Library. Go west on McAllister to Arguello, where you may want to stop at the deli and get a great hand-carved turkey sandwich. Go south to Fulton and find the old railroad stop at 7th Ave (see p. 28).

This neighborhood saw a housing boom after '06, when most of the city was devastated. By the 1920s houses had just about filled out the entire distance between Arguello and Ocean Beach. Though Geary and Clement became the chief commercial streets of the Richmond, Balboa Street is, I think, a better example of the mixture of residential and business life. Keep following the yellow track if it's Sunday, stop at the Russian Evangelical House on Balboa and 14th Ave. and venture inside. Farther on you will find Balboa's main commercial district, between 34th and 39th Avenues, punctuated by Colette Crutcher's Streetscape sculptures. Note the Balboa Theater and stop inside Marla's Bakery for a great snack. Finally, go up the hill to the Cliff House, look out at Seal Rocks, then end at Sutro Heights Park and enjoy the great view south from there before heading back to Geary and the 38 bus.

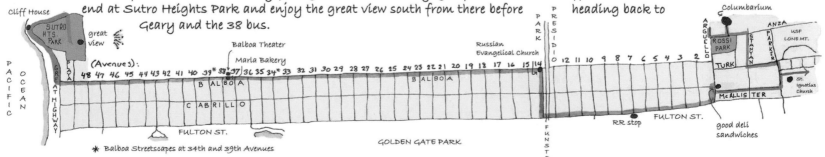

* Balboa Streetscapes at 34th and 39th Avenues

WALK #3: Lake Street, Sea Cliff and the stairs on 32nd and California

<u>START</u>: Arguello & Washington
<u>END</u>: 32nd Ave & California
<u>DISTANCE</u>: about 3 miles
<u>RETURN</u>: #1 California going
             east back to Arguello

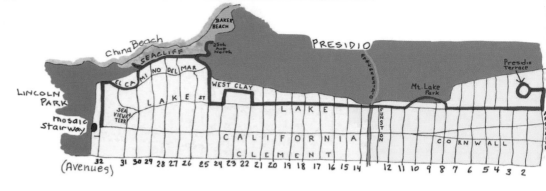

Start by making a loop around Presidio Terrace before turning right, then right again onto Lake Street. At 8th Ave detour into Mountain Lake Park, a natural lake, and enjoy the paths and green-ery. Continue up Lake, detouring again at West Clay, then walk back to Lake and over to 25th, where you turn right and follow the route to Sea Cliff and the end of

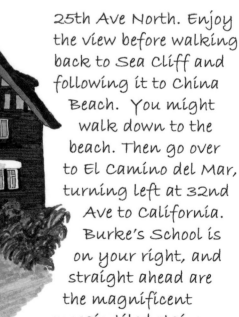

25th Ave North. Enjoy the view before walking back to Sea Cliff and following it to China Beach. You might walk down to the beach. Then go over to El Camino del Mar, turning left at 32nd Ave to California. Burke's School is on your right, and straight ahead are the magnificent mosaic-tiled stairs that lead up to Lin-coln Park. (see p. 94)

Presidio Terrace house and Temple Emanu-el

WALK #4: Ingleside Terraces to West Portal

START: Ocean Ave & Victoria St
END: West Portal, somewhere
DISTANCT: about 3 miles
RETURN: K Street car back to start (or walk)

** Be sure to wander a bit
as you explore these
neighborhoods!

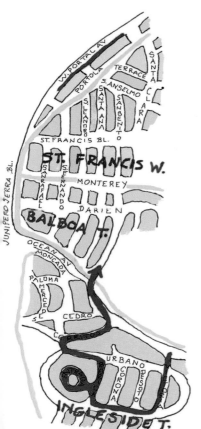

These neighborhoods (Ingleside Terraces, Balboa Terrace, St. Francis Wood and West Portal) mostly developed after the completion of the Twin Peaks tunnel in 1917.

INGLESIDE TERRACES became a part of the SF landscape with the opening of an oval race track on what is now Urbano Drive. On the track's opening day, Nov. 28, 1895, almost 12,000 people showed up on a drizzly afternoon even though there was strong competition from the Cal-Stanford game that day over on Haight St. (they tied). Horse and car racing (i.e. gambling) ended after the '06 earthquake when the space became a refugee camp for homeless San Franciscans. Another of this neighborhood's features is the 1913 sundial on Entrada, 28 feet high with a clock 34 feet in diameter surrounding it, celebrating the 4 seasons & the 4 ages of man.

BALBOA TERRACE became a residential neighborhood later, from 1920-27.

ST. FRANCIS WOOD is an example of a planned "suburban, forested community of family homes nestled in an urban setting," according to Duncan McDuffy, the real estate developer who broke the SF tradition of 25-foot lots with houses sitting cheek by jowl. Frederick Olmsted, who had designed Central Park in New York City, planned & landscaped the new neighborhood, the only one in the city that has more green than cement. Neighborhood residents must pay monthly dues to keep up its common areas.

Continue to WEST PORTAL, where you can shop, eat and view the tunnel that made all this possible.

WALK #5: Diamond Heights and Glen Park

<u>START:</u> Diamond Heights Blvd. and Red Rock
<u>END:</u> Diamond St and Wilder
<u>DISTANCE:</u> about 3 miles
<u>RETURN:</u> 52 bus back uphill (get it at Wilder and Diamond)

This walk will take you through the (relatively) new and the more historic. Diamond Heights, which was the city's first redevelopment neighborhood in the 1960s, and the older (back to the 1890s) Glen Park, a charming enclave with attractive houses on winding streets and country lanes following the hill's contours down to the BART station on Diamond Street. Do walk Penny and Poppy Lanes on your trek down, and do enjoy the views of Glen Canyon before you finish up on Diamond and Chenery. Reward yourself by trying the popular Mexican restaurant and visiting the Canyon Market, a neighborhood icon, before you catch the bus back up the hill.

WALK #6: 24th Street (Noe Valley and the Mission)

<u>START:</u> 24th and Douglass
<u>END:</u> 24th and Potrero
<u>DISTANCE:</u> about 2 miles
<u>RETURN:</u> 48 bus back to start

The highlights of this sublime walk down 24th Street in the heart of Noe Valley and the Mission are many. Enjoy the shops and cafes as you walk by them. 24th Street has an excellent bookstore (Folio), a chocolate shop (Chocolate Covered) and any number of nice places to stop and eat. But it's the murals on this walk that make it memorable. Take a detour down Balmy Alley, Lucky Alley, Cypress Alley, the parking lot of Capp Street, the House of Brakes, and even McDonald's at 24th and Mission. Balmy Alley comes just before you get to Harrison Street.

**and do stop at Humphry Slocumb (named after Mrs. Slocumb on the hysterically funny series <u>Are You Being Served?</u>) on 24th and Harrison. I recommend the Vietnamese coffee ice cream.

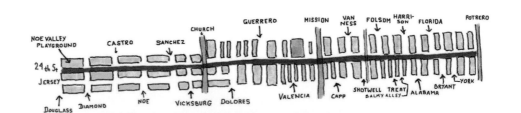

WALK #7: Marina to Ft. Point

START: Ft. Point (get there on the 28 bus & walk down the hill)
END: in the Marina, somewhere
DISTANCE: up to you...
RETURN: use the 28 bus if you need transportation back

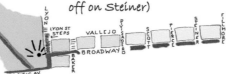

I recommend starting at Ft. Point and the Golden Gate Bridge in order to enjoy the great views of the city from the promenade. I always get a kick out of the dogs, kids and families romping on the beach at Crissy Field. Don't forget to look back at the bridge and its 746-foot towers. Its 80,000 miles of cable provide the strength and flexibility to withstand fierce Pacific storms and major earthquakes. The bridge was completed in 1937. Then I recommend walking past the St. Francis Yacht Club to the Wave Organ, an acoustic sculpture built in 1986 by the Exploratorium. Continue to the Maybeck-designed Palace of Fine Arts, built for the Panama-Pacific International Exposition in 1915, and then into the streets of the Marina, a neighborhood built mostly after the Fair, mostly completed by 1930. Find a place to have a snack or a meal on Chestnut Street. You can catch the 28 bus on Lombard Street and get back to your starting point.

WALK #8: Gold Coast to Crissy Field and the Presidio Cemetery

START: Broadway & Fillmore Streets
END: S.F. National Cemetery
DISTANCE: about 4 miles
RETURN: 28 bus to Fillmore, then transfer to 22 (Fillmore) bus back to Broadway (get off on Steiner)

This walk takes you past the mansions on Broadway to the Lyon Street steps (great view). Before heading downhill on Lovers' Lane, note the shingled houses built along the Presidio wall between 1902 and 1913, designed by such notables as Bernard Maybeck, Julia Morgan, Willis Polk, Ernest Coxhead, Albert Farr and William Knowles. Lovers' Lane is a peaceful walk through the eucalyptus forest (non-native) to the Officers' Club and the parade ground. If it's Sunday between March and November, you can enjoy the vast variety of food from Off the Grid. The Disney Museum in the Montgomery Street Barracks is worth a visit. Finally, head to the cemetery, one of only three-plus cemeteries left in the city (others are the Columbarium and Mission Dolores as well as the tiny, one-grave cemetery at the First Unitarian Church on Franklin Street). Buried here are soldiers from a surprising number of wars. See how many different conflicts are represented...

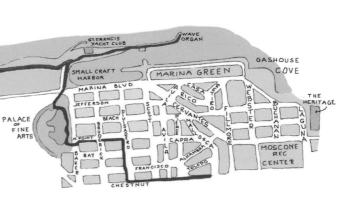

WALK #9: Market Street

START: Castro and Market
END: Ferry Plaza
DISTANCE: 3+ miles
RETURN: K, L, M or T street car

Wander Market Street from the flamboyant Castro past the changing mid-Market area into the financial district and finally Ferry Plaza. Get distracted often, going off route to check out, maybe, Mission Dolores, City Hall, the Opera House, Davies Symphony Hall, Union Square and the street art along upper Mission Street. Good stops along Market include:

1. Twitter Headquarters: 10th and Market (fancy market inside)
2. Lotta's Fountain (Kearny & Market), honors Lotta Crabtree
3. Monadnock Building: 685 Market - murals inside of well-known San Franciscans - how many can you guess?
4. Palace Hotel: Maxfield Parrish mural in bar
5. Hayes Valley: roughly between Octavia & Franklin, Grove & Fell - shopping, eating, culture, lots of it
6. Hobart Building: 582 Market
7. Crocker Galleria: 50 Post Street - go upstairs to the roof garden
8. PGE Building: 245 Market
9. Matson Building: 215 Market
10. Hearst Building: 3rd & Market
11. Federal Reserve Bank: between Spear and Main Streets

12. Audiffred Building: on The Embarcadero off Market Street; earthquake survivor; look for chef statue on mansard roof
13. Vaillancourt Fountain: at Justin Herman Plaza - controversial!
14. Ferry Plaza - what a treat: food, kitchen stuff, books, places to sit and read or talk with a friend

**There's lots more: explore as much as you have time for. and use your smart phone to look up the history of places you want to know more about.

WALK #10: Twin Peaks, the Haight and Cole Valley

START: Clarendon and Twin Peaks   **END:** Clayton & Ashbury
DISTANCE: about 3 miles   **RETURN:** 33 bus (or walk)

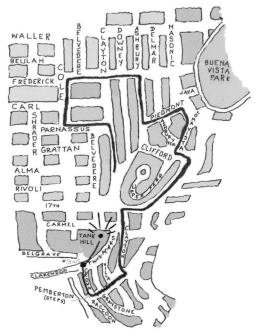

This walk will take you through some of the most scenic & historic parts of the city. From the start, walk over to Tank Hill & climb the path to the top so you can take in the incredible view of the Marin Headlands and the Golden Gate Bridge. Then go down the hill to Crown Terrace and follow it briefly to Pemberton. Walk down the steps, past the neatly tended gardens that look very English. At Clayton look across the street to the garden planted and maintained by a generous neighbor. Follow the route on the map through the Upper Haight and then into Cole Valley. You'll find lots of eating choices on Cole Street, but save some room for ice cream at the old-fashioned parlor between Frederick and Carl. When you go by the Cole Valley car repair shop, don't miss the whimsical mural.

WALK #!!: Golden Gate Park

START: Arguello & Fulton (start early!)   **END:** Beach Chalet   **DISTANCE:** 5-6 miles
RETURN: walk north to Fulton, take the #5 bus back to Arguello (east)

This walk is rather long, but you'll see Golden Gate Park from its more "cultured" east end to its more wild west end. Don't miss the Conservatory of Flowers, the Academy of Sciences, the DeYoung Museum (excellent cafeteria) or the Japanese tea garden. Take a quiet walk around Stow Lake, before going on to Spreckels Lake with its model sailboats making their way across the placid water. A bison paddock houses a couple of phlegmatic bison, reminiscent of our past. Keep walking past the windmills, one of which was a gift from Queen Wilhelmina of Holland. Finish at Beach Chalet with a meal upstairs after you enjoy the W.P.A. murals on the ground floor.

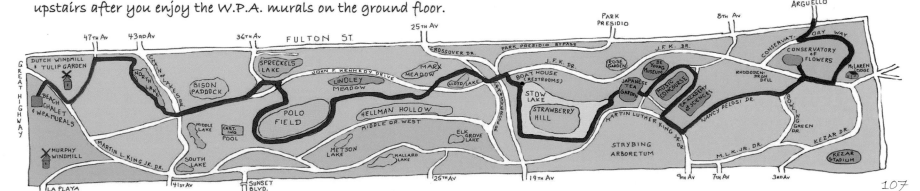

WALK #12: Valencia Street

START: Valencia & McCoppin   **END:** Valencia & Mission
DISTANCE: 2-3 miles, depending on side trips
RETURN: 14 Mission bus back to 14th Street

**Don't miss the Friends School at Clinton Park,
former Levi's factory

This is a walk through the heart of the Mission. Start at the north end of Valencia Street under the freeway next to the dog park on your left. If you go left onto Duboce, you'll see a skateboard park with lots of daredevils to wow you. Back to Valencia: This neighborhood bears little resemblance to the one my father-in-law had his real estate office on years ago. Now it is a tony place with world class restaurants, great murals, coffee shops (don't miss Ritual), the very popular Bi-Rite Market and ice cream parlor (across the street from each other), 826 Valencia (a pirate shop fronting for a mentoring center helping at-risk kids), a bookstore with a uniquely decorated exterior (Dog Eared at 20th and Valencia), a theater (Marsh), and more. You might stop in at Hog and Rocks, an upscale bar with unusual drinks, on Lexington and San Carlos. Don't miss the Women's Center at Linda and Lapidge - go inside to enjoy the brightly painted stairway. The mostly political murals on Clarion Alley change often, depending on the season. But the crown jewel is Balmy Alley, with its murals that depict social and political issues, especially of the Hispanic population of the neighborhood.

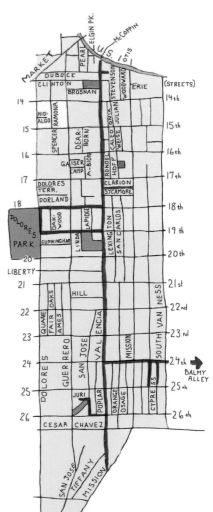

Victorians on Valencia at Liberty Street

WALK #13: Nob Hill and Chinatown

START: Grace Cathedral (California & Taylor)
END: Portsmouth Square (Kearny betw. Washington & Clay)
RETURN: #1 California bus at Sacramento & Kearny

This walk will be without a specific route, only recommended
stops. Chinatown is full of surprises, so you should explore it
on your own. But don't miss: Grace Cathedral (labyrinths, Ghiberti doors and stained glass
windows), Huntington Park across the street, the Mark Hopkins Hotel (Room of the Dons with
murals by Maynard Dixon & Frank Van Sloun), the
Fairmont Hotel, and in Chinatown: Ross Alley,
Wentworth Alley, Waverly Place, Spofford Alley,
the Chinese Historical Museum at 965 Clay, and
Portsmouth Square (site of the first public school
in SF - but though it was Chinatown, Chinese
were not allowed to attend!). Look for herbal
medicine shops, musicians and
musical instrument shops,
mah jongg games, temples
and tongs. Take in the
street life. Find a fortune
cookie maker. It's all like
visiting a foreign country.

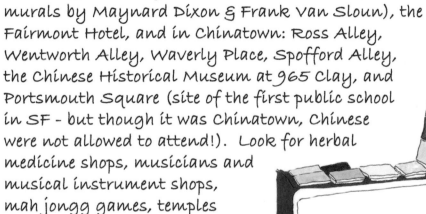

109

WALK #14: The Haight and beyond

__START:__ Haight and Stanyan   __END:__ Zen Center?   __DISTANCE:__ about 3-4 miles
__RETURN:__ #71 bus

Not to be missed is a walk through the (now mostly) historic Haight. It still has the aura of quirkiness if less of the counter-culture rebellion of the '60s & '70s. Walk east on Haight, enjoy the way the shops are adorned. Work your way to Alamo Square, surrounded by turn of the (last) century houses, including the famous Painted Ladies. If you are feeling ambitious, continue on to the Zen Center at 300 Page between Laguna & Buchanan; maybe even back to Hayes Street down into Hayes Valley. Treat yourself to some wonderful chocolate at Christopher Elbow (401 Hayes) before getting on the #71 bus back to Stanyan. Some highlights:

1. Haight Street shops (Amoeba Music, Roberts Hardware, and more)
2. 636 Cole (where Chas. Manson had his nest with his harem)
3. Haight-Ashbury Free Clinic at 558 Clayton, still operating
4. 710 Ashbury (Grateful Dead house)
5. 1 Broderick (Huckleberry House at the top, refuge for runaways)

Use your gadget to look up the more detailed histories

**recommended reading:
<u>Season of the Witch</u>, by
David Talbot, for background
on the Haight in the '60s & '70s

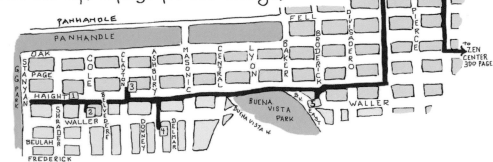

WALK #15: North Beach & Telegraph Hill

No route here; it's another self-discovery walk, but I hope you visit all the red dotted spots. Wander around North Beach and allow yourself to be tempted into one of the cafes or restaurants. I love to do lunch at House, near the south end of Grant Ave. Visit Washington Square (morning is good because you can catch local Chinese doing exercises), Sts. Peter & Paul Church, St. Francis Chapel on Vallejo & Columbus, the Maybeck Bldg. on Stockton just north of Washington Sq. (see p. 4). Climb up Telegraph Hill to Coit Tower. On Wednesday mornings you can take a free City Guide tour of the W.P.A. Depression-era murals inside and even of those behind the closed door upstairs: one depicts Eleanor Roosevelt, one a Stanford-Cal football game. Walk down the Filbert Street steps all the way to The Embarcadero, but not before you check out Alta Street and Calhoun Place, their houses perched precariously on the hill. Finish going down the steps - your legs might complain, but they'll get over it. When you get to the bottom, you might call a Lyft or Uber car to get you back to your start.

Edwardian doorway

111

WALK #16: Russian Hill

START: Polk & Chestnut
END: Polk & Green
DISTANCE: 3+ miles
RETURN: #19 Polk (or walk)

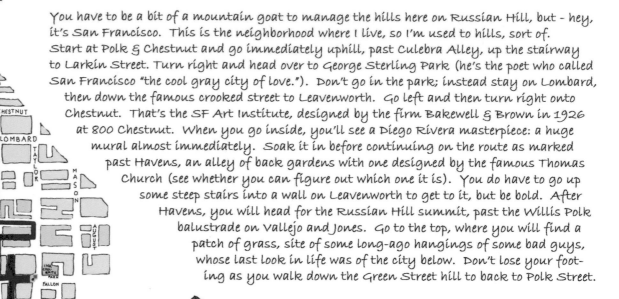

You have to be a bit of a mountain goat to manage the hills here on Russian Hill, but - hey, it's San Francisco. This is the neighborhood where I live, so I'm used to hills, sort of. Start at Polk & Chestnut and go immediately uphill, past Culebra Alley, up the stairway to Larkin Street. Turn right and head over to George Sterling Park (he's the poet who called San Francisco "the cool gray city of love."). Don't go in the park; instead stay on Lombard, then down the famous crooked street to Leavenworth. Go left and then turn right onto Chestnut. That's the SF Art Institute, designed by the firm Bakewell & Brown in 1926 at 800 Chestnut. When you go inside, you'll see a Diego Rivera masterpiece: a huge mural almost immediately. Soak it in before continuing on the route as marked past Havens, an alley of back gardens with one designed by the famous Thomas Church (see whether you can figure out which one it is). You do have to go up some steep stairs into a wall on Leavenworth to get to it, but be bold. After Havens, you will head for the Russian Hill summit, past the Willis Polk balustrade on Vallejo and Jones. Go to the top, where you will find a patch of grass, site of some long-ago hangings of some bad guys, whose last look in life was of the city below. Don't lose your footing as you walk down the Green Street hill to back to Polk Street.

little houses on Russell Street

WALK #17: Third Street

START: 3rd and King Streets   **END:** 3rd and Jerrold
DISTANCE: 5+ miles   **RETURN:** 3rd Street rail

This walk is a bit long, so start early and take a lot of breaks. Begin at AT&T Park venue of our hometown heroes, the Giants. Spend some time on the portwalk, the walkway along the bay, inbibing their rich history of baseball here in SF. They moved from New York in 1958, but until 2000 spent most of their years playing at frigid Candle-Stick. Then AT&T was built, right on the bay with view of the Bay Bridge and the East Bay hills to enjoy. Home runs sometimes go into McCovey Cove, earning them the name "splash hits" and a permanent place in the record book. When you've had enough baseball atmosphere, head across the drawbridge to Mission Bay, the city's newest neighborhood. UCSF is here, and along with it Mark Benioff's Children's Hospital, several biotech firms, a Kaiser Hospital and many doctors' offices. Continue south; when you get to Mariposa Street, turn right and walk over to Minnesota and turn left. As you walk down Minnesota, you'll see several restored $572 catalog houses from Dogpatch's early history, Esprit Park, a gift from its founders, Susie and Doug Tompkins, who created the clothing success story in the '60s, and an old schoolhouse, maybe the first one in San Francisco.

At 22nd Street you'll see a yellow and green painted Victorian, Piccino's, a terrific lunch place. After lunch you can decide between Just For You (great beignets, loved by the Hell's Angels, whose headquarters are around the corner on Tennessee Street) and Mr. and Mrs. Miscellaneous, where you can get unusual flavors of home-made ice cream. Walk on south to Cargo Way, go left and head to Heron's Head (page 81), the eco-friendly bird sanctuary on a spit of land shaped like a heron's head. Walk out to the end of the point and enjoy the view of the hills of Hayward across the bay. Go back to 3rd Street, turn left and walk to Flora Grubb, a garden of Eden for plant and garden lovers. You've done a lot!

Heron's Head
oystercatcher

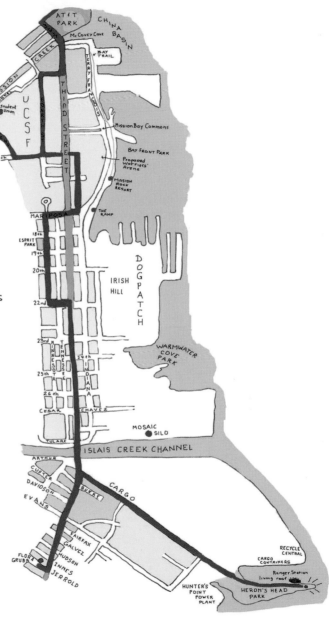

WALK #18: The Fillmore, Japantown and more

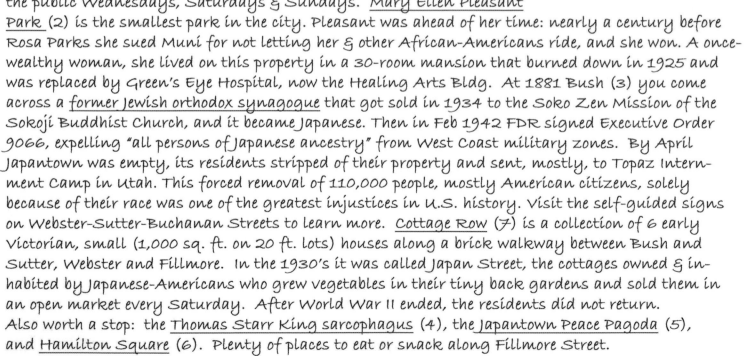

<u>START:</u> Franklin & Washington (Haas-Lilienthal house)
<u>END:</u> somewhere on Fillmore Street
<u>DISTANCE:</u> about 4 miles with lots of backtracking
<u>RETURN:</u> #10 bus (Fillmore & Washington) to Franklin

The <u>Haas-Lilienthal house</u> (1) is an 1886 Queen Anne Victorian, built in the 1870s and a testament to the heritage of San Francisco's Jewish community. Today it is open to the public Wednesdays, Saturdays & Sundays. <u>Mary Ellen Pleasant Park</u> (2) is the smallest park in the city. Pleasant was ahead of her time: nearly a century before Rosa Parks she sued Muni for not letting her & other African-Americans ride, and she won. A once-wealthy woman, she lived on this property in a 30-room mansion that burned down in 1925 and was replaced by Green's Eye Hospital, now the Healing Arts Bldg. At 1881 Bush (3) you come across a <u>former Jewish orthodox synagogue</u> that got sold in 1934 to the Soko Zen Mission of the Sokoji Buddhist Church, and it became Japanese. Then in Feb 1942 FDR signed Executive Order 9066, expelling "all persons of Japanese ancestry" from West Coast military zones. By April Japantown was empty, its residents stripped of their property and sent, mostly, to Topaz Internment Camp in Utah. This forced removal of 110,000 people, mostly American citizens, solely because of their race was one of the greatest injustices in U.S. history. Visit the self-guided signs on Webster-Sutter-Buchanan Streets to learn more. <u>Cottage Row</u> (7) is a collection of 6 early Victorian, small (1,000 sq. ft. on 20 ft. lots) houses along a brick walkway between Bush and Sutter, Webster and Fillmore. In the 1930's it was called Japan Street, the cottages owned & inhabited by Japanese-Americans who grew vegetables in their tiny back gardens and sold them in an open market every Saturday. After World War II ended, the residents did not return.
Also worth a stop: the <u>Thomas Starr King sarcophagus</u> (4), the <u>Japantown Peace Pagoda</u> (5), and <u>Hamilton Square</u> (6). Plenty of places to eat or snack along Fillmore Street.

WALK #19: Bernal Heights

START: Alabama & Precita Ave   END: Cortland Ave OR Mission St
DISTANCE: 2.4 miles, depending on sidetrips
RETURN: 24 bus on Cortland to Mission (transfer to 14 Mission) OR
       67 Bernal Heights bus on Folsom back to Precita Park

A former student of mine described Bernal Heights, where he lives with his family, as a place with lots of stairways, dogs and families, both gay and straight, but all with kids. Bernal Heights has 4 parks within its boundaries. It has many very steep streets that wind so much walking around the block is often an exercise in frustration. A mixed neighborhood economically, it goes from increasingly expensive homes to public housing on Alemany and Appleton. But I love the neighborhood. Its cafes, especially around Precita Park, are welcoming and full of families. The shops and eateries along Cortland Ave welcome visitors as well as locals. But mostly, it's called "Heights" for good reason: a walk up Ripley Street is a serious work-out. Wander around, even if that means not following the red lined route. Enjoy the neat, charming homes along the way.

I find it endlessly amusing that a little dog will charge a big one, apparently oblivious to his obvious disadvantage in combat.

WALK #20: Cayuga Park (Mission Terrace)

<u>START</u>: Ocean & San Jose Avenues
<u>END</u>: Ocean Ave & Alemany
<u>DISTANCE</u>: about 3 miles
<u>RETURN</u>: 49 Mission bus

This is a real treat: Walk down Cayuga Ave. past Balboa High School (page 71) to Cayuga Park. This charming garden/ park is filled with wooden carvings by Demetrios Braceros, the former gardener here. They are whimsical, spiritual, mythic, - and are utterly delightful. Demetrios had worked in a law office, but quit when he realized sitting behind a desk didn't suit him. He went to work for Park and Rec, requesting a park in need of a makeover. He got Cayuga Park, a messy hangout for kids up to no good. He cleaned it up and started carving; the rest is history.

The murals on Mission Street nearby are all worth a look, especially the bakery and Central Drug Store on Santa Rosa Avenue.